THE BALLAD OF THE S.
AND OTHER V

ACKNOWLEDGEMENT
*I want to thank the artists who have recorded my lyrics
over the years, especially Jackie and Roy who were the first*

STEVE ALLEN ED AMES ANAMARI
CHET BAKER SHIRLEY BASSEY TONY BENNETT
JACKIE CAIN IAN CARMICHAEL BETTY CARTER
DIANNA CARROLL JUNE CHRISTY PETULA CLARK
BILL CUNNINGHAM CHRIS CONNOR MILES DAVIS
BOB DOROUGH GIL EVANS GEORGIE FAME
THE FIFTH DIMENSION ELLA FITZGERALD
ROBERTA FLACK STAN GETZ DAVEY GRAHAM
RICHARD HAYES BUD HERRMANN DAVE HOWARD
HARRY JAMES FRAN JEFFRIES ROGER KELLAWAY
IRENE KRAL ROY KRAL CLEO LAINE LOIS LANE
RAMSEY LEWIS JULIE LONDON CARMAN MACRAE
MIRIAM MEKEBA HERBIE MANN ROD McKUEN
HELEN MERRILL MABEL MERCER CHAD MITCHELL
LIBBY MORRIS MARK MURPHY ANTHONY NEWLEY
ANITA O'DAY ROBIE PORTER RUTH PRICE
ANITA RAY RITA REYS ZOOT SIMS CAROL SIMPSON
JOHN SIMON SPANKY AND OUR GANG
STANLEY TURRENTINE SARAH VAUGHAN
NANCY WILSON JERRI WINTERS
MARGARET WHITING TOMMY WOLF

To my collaborators for the music that made it all happen:

STEVE ALLEN BOB DOROUGH GEORGIE FAME
RICHARD RODNEY BENNETT TONY KINSEY
ROY KRAL DUDLEY MOORE LEE POCKRESS
JOHN SIMON TOM SPRINGFIELD ALEC WILDER
and special thanks to the one who got me started, TOMMY WOLF

*Grateful thanks to The Richmond Organisation TRO,
Empress Music, and Wolf-Mills Music for permission to
reprint the lyrics to "Ballad of the Sad Young Men"
(Empress Music) ; "A Man Who Used to Be" and
"Am I O.K.?" (TRO) ; "Spring Can Really Hang You
Up the Most" (Wolf-Mills)*

The Ballad of the Sad Young Men
and other Verse

FRAN LANDESMAN

POLYTANTRIC PRESS

159 WARDOUR STREET

LONDON W1

DEDICATION

To all the sad young men

© *Frances Landesman*
First published in Great Britain by
the Polytantric Press, 1975
Second Edition 1978
ISBN 0 905150 007
Printed in Great Britain by
Latimer Trend & Company Ltd Plymouth

CONTENTS

PEOPLE I'VE KNOWN

MOSTLY ME

PEOPLE I'VE KNOWN

THE BALLAD OF THE SAD YOUNG MEN

All the sad young men
Sitting in the bars
Knowing neon lights
Missing all the stars

All the sad young men
Drifting through the town
Drinking up the night
Trying not to drown

Sing a song of sad young men
Glasses full of rye
All the news is bad again
Kiss your dreams goodbye

All the sad young men
Seek a certain smile
Someone they can hold
For a little while

Tired little girl
Does the best she can
Trying to be gay
For a sad young man

Autumn turns the leaves to gold
Slowly dies the heart
Sad young men are growing old
That's the cruellest part

While a grimy moon
Watches from above
All the sad young men
Play at making love

Misbegotten moon
Shine for sad young men
Let your gentle light
Guide them home again
All the sad young men

BOGIE

He gets paid to take chances
And he knows how to deal
He wears gloves made of leather
And a smile made of steel

With his five o'clock shadow
And his heart of pure gold
He will always be Bogie
And he'll never grow old

She's a girl who's in trouble
All her nights are like years
She wears dresses of satin
And a necklace of tears

She was Ida or Ingrid
Till along came Bacall
But he'll always be Bogie
And he's king of them all

He makes love with a wisecrack
'Cause he's wise to her schemes
So "Here's looking at you, kid"
He still walks in our dreams

Watch him knock back a bourbon
While she straightens her seams
He will always be Bogie
And he walks in my dreams

"SHE" (for Hanja)

She so pretty, She so crazy
So delightful and so lazy
She make pictures, She make babies
All her life is full of "maybes"

She can light your darkest hours
She got visions, She got powers
Everything She makes unravels
Got no money, still She travels

She play cinderella
In fantastic rags
Pretty girls beside her
Look like well-dressed hags

She got beauty mixed with sadness
She make magic, She make madness
Read your hand or cure your fever
But her lovers always leave her

She so lovely, She so vicious
She do cooking so delicious
I could kill her, I could kiss her
When She go away I miss her

BAD PENNY

You're an elegant artist
You make pictures of pain
You can give and take it
With a smile like cocaine

I keep trying to lose you
I'm afraid of your schemes
But you've captured my fancy
And invaded my dreams

Bad Penny, always turning up
Bad Penny, madness in your cup
Uncanny in your satin gown
Bad Penny, bright satanic clown

I can't resist your silky style
The diamonds in your head
And though you are a superstar
You bring me tea in bed

You appeared as Ophelia
When our friendship began
Then the next time I saw you
You were dressed as a man

With a wonderful swagger
And a twirl of your cane
You make everything sparkle
You make madness seem sane

Sweet Jenny used to be your friend
You left her nothing in the end
Bad Penny, lovely, spoiled and smart
Bad Penny, will you break my heart?

BURNED

He was steely, he was salty
He was crazy, he was wise
There are two holes in the carpet
That he burned there with his eyes
Just staring at the carpet
He burned it with his eyes
With his eyes, with his eyes
With his holy madman's eyes

He was with me all one summer
On the California sands
There are two scars on my shoulders
Where he burned me with his hands
He touched my skin so gently
He burned me with his hands
With his hands, with his hands
With his holy con man's hands

He's an eloquent liar, he's a dreamer in red
He's a teacher on fire and a killer in bed
He keeps writing me letters from wherever he lands
And the pain gets no better but I can understand

He got restless in the autumn
And he drifted toward the south
There are marks upon the pillow
Where he burned it with his mouth
He left my mind on fire
He burned me with his mouth
With his mouth, with his mouth
With his holy poet's mouth
And his holy con man's hands
And his holy madman's eyes

WHAT AM I DOIN' WITH YOU?

I'm always cold, you're always hot
I'm all worn out when you are not
I sit and watch, you want to dance
I play it safe, you take a chance
Oh baby, what am I doin' with you?

You like the woods, I like the town
You're mostly up, I'm mostly down
I sip champagne, you guzzle beer
But there's some reason why you're here
Oh baby, what am I doin' with you?

You want to go, I'd rather not
I'm always cold, you're always hot
But when you're hot and holding me
Somehow we manage to agree
Oh baby, what would I do without you?

DO YOU REMEMBER?

We've known each other ages and over oceans too
And in the times we never meet I often think of you
The last time that I saw you you were leaving for the coast
You came into my bed that night just like a gentle ghost

Do you remember?
You rubbed my back and stroked my hair
But in the morning
It seemed like you were never there

You left me in the kitchen and you muttered something dumb
And no one there would ever guess how close we almost
  come
The songs we made together had a flavour of their own
But they were always second to the songs you made alone

Do you remember?
You rubbed my back and stroked my hair
But in the morning
It seemed like you were never there
Seemed just like you were never there at all

THE PRINCESS FROM FLATBUSH

She's got a bracelet from Cartiers and beauty and wit
She's got a dozen new lovers but none of them fit
She's got two eyes like black olives and very nice tits
She's just a Princess from Flatbush who stays at the Ritz

She came a long way from Brooklyn without a career
She's busy hiding and seeking and fighting her fear
She's got a house on the lakefront, a plum tree with plums
But all her elegant dinners still taste of the slums

She settled in Geneva beside a crooked man
Goes skiing in the winter and keeps her perfect tan
The crooked man has vanished and left her lots of bread
She's reading Krishnamurti to straighten out her head

She studied chess with a master and soon had him beat
But all her really good gambits she learned in the street
I go to faraway places and find far-out chums
But I remember her kisses that taste of the slums

THE PRINCE OF SWORDS

Self-crowned protector of the wounded
Self-crowned destroyer of the strong
What am I doing in your movie?
How long, oh love, how long?

Many are ready to acclaim you
Many will follow where you lead
How can you keep your wine unwatered
With all those loves to feed

Once you appeared in armour shining
Once I was captured by your smile
Now I can see you as my killer
The jury at my trial

Do you remember winter landscapes
Nutcakes and figs and china tea?
Fire-lit your hands were warm and gentle
Your sword was sheathed in me

You try to train me like a falcon
I have my sky dream to protect
So you select another lover
Who shows you more respect

I could have stood your other lovers
I could have let you travel free
If you had found in all your bounty
One special place for me

I'll fly away before I'm broken
Leaving you satin and a song
Self-crowned protector of the wounded
Self-crowned destroyer of the strong

SINBAD APOLLO

Sinbad the sailor signs himself Apollo
Making his migrations like a golden swallow

Sinbad the madman, who can solve his mystery
Smiling at the snowflakes, giggling at history?

Sinbad has landed, all the girls enjoy him
All the sinners love him, nothing can destroy him

Sinbad is good times. Sunshine doesn't hurt you
Though he always leaves you, he will not desert you

Where Sinbad rested funny dreams will follow
Sinbad the mystery signs himself Apollo

BOY

Naked boy in a green feather boa
Lit by gas fire
Did I dream you?

Smiling shy on the Indian pillows
Pale hair shining
Please remember

Did you come on some tornado
From the land of Oz
All decked out in emerald feathers
Stranded in this cloudy country?

Were you one of my inventions?
Whisper to me now
Did we ever melt together
By the pink light of the gas fire?

Naked boy in a green feather boa
Paint your eyelids
Let me dream you
One more time

SON OF A FAMOUS FATHER

You might have been a writer, musician or a saint
You might have been an actor or told your tale in paint
But now you're just a hustler who travels with the tide
An easy riding con man who never even tried

Son of a famous father, you work hard having fun
Everyone hurries forward to meet your father's son
You started in your childhood to play a special game
Bearing a special burden, your famous father's name

The people ask you questions about your father's life
His habits and his pastimes, his crazy second wife
You answer them with patience, supply the missing link
The only thing you ask them is buy another drink

Women are what you win at, you never do them right
Watching the way they wind up is not a pretty sight
Women can hear your nightmares, they love the games you
    play
Somehow you must destroy them before they slip away

Whenever you get busted somebody bails you out
With all your charm and talent you only fuck about
You can't ignore his footsteps on any side of town
He's too much to live up to and so you live him down

You can't avoid his shadow no matter what you do
Though he was loved by many he had no time for you
How could you ever touch him when all is said and done?
Son of a famous father you load your father's gun

MERCEDES-BENZ

He won the Pulitzer Prize and the Oscar
A writer can't do much better than that
And his novels are known from Osh-Kosh to Rome
Seems like success just ain't where it's at

How come it all turns into ashes so many times?
How come the rainbow turns black where it ends?
How come we read in the papers so many times
They found him slumped in the seat of his Mercedes-Benz?

If there is one thing we envy it's talent
To make a record like Bobby or Paul
And we love them so much we'd die for their touch
But all that love don't touch them at all

How come that singer in the spotlight is hooked on junk
When he's got two million lovers and friends?
How come with all of that talent his light went out?
They found him slumped in the seat of his Mercedes-Benz

I hope you're not expecting an answer
'Cause I'm as hungry and star-struck as you
I know about all the strain and boredom and pain
But I still can't believe that it's true

Just let me have my ride on that rainbow
And I won't worry 'bout where it all ends
'Cause I can handle that speed so you ain't gonna read
"They found him slumped in the seat of his Mercedes-Benz"

MYSTERY MAN

I wish you'd tell me what you want and who you are
I wonder just what kind of life you're looking for
At times you seem so full of light, so bright and pure
I don't believe you're playing games but I'm not sure

You speak in accents of affection
But never give your heart away
Are people coins in your collection?
And will you spend them all some day?

I'm vain enough to think that I could find a cure
For maladies your mind has made, but I'm not sure
You tell me how the friends you have are using you
Perhaps you feel that way because you do it too

You seem to thrive on complications
I have to smile when you complain
Do you invent these situations?
Is it your stars that are to blame?

I've heard that there are one or two who you've betrayed
You say that other hands upset the plans you made
I'm half afraid that knowing you may leave a scar
I wonder if you know yourself just who you are

SHE USED TO SING
(ANOTHER LOOK AT MOTHER)

Hard to believe that she used to sing
When she tucked you into bed
Hard to believe that she used to laugh
And her hair was sunset red

Hard to believe she was ever young
That she tasted any joy
Hard to believe that her heart could melt
In the arms of any boy

Her life was not a hard one
She lived quite well
And why she's grown so bitter
Is more than I can tell

Hard to believe that you loved her so
For she's grown so mean and small
Seeing her now you just can't believe
That she ever sang at all

SISTER SONG

You asked me to be your mirror
I looked into your eyes
We both saw our own reflections
In hell and paradise

I wanted to be your sister
Perhaps in truth I was
The magical tea we swallowed
Made rainbows of our clothes

I saw how your face was fragile
Down to it's ivory bone
I saw how the pain you suffered
Was very like my own

I saw how the years would treat you
I saw how your eyes would age
I knew how you'd burn to ashes
With happiness and rage

I saw you as some bright angel
And just as surely damned
You asked me to be your mirror
And now in truth I am

A MAN WHO USED TO BE

Would you dance with a man
Who used to be handsome
Used to be dashing
Used to be brave
Now he isn't so old
But somehow he's slipping
Still he's got something
Someone could save

Would you dance with a man
Who used to be lucky
Someone or something
Pitched him a curve
Now he's stuck in a rut
Down at the office
Drinking his lunches
Losing his nerve

Would you dance with a man
Who watches old movies
Dreams about glory
Longs for the sea
If you fancy a man
Who used to be handsome
Used to be fearless and free
Then this is the moment
If ever there was one
To look for the man who was me

MOSTLY ME

SPRING CAN REALLY HANG YOU
UP THE MOST

Spring this year has got me feeling
Like a horse that never left the post
I lie in my room staring up at the ceiling
Spring can really hang you up the most

College boys are writing sonnets
In the tender passion they're engrossed
But I'm on the shelf with last year's Easter bonnets
Spring can really hang you up the most

All afternoon those birds twitter-twit
I know the tune "This is love! This is it!"
Spring came along, season of song
Full of sweet promise but something wrong

Doctors once prescribed a tonic
Sulphur and molasses was the dose
Didn't help a bit. My condition must be chronic
Spring can really hang you up the most

All alone the party's over
Old man Winter was a gracious host
But when you keep praying for snow to hide the clover
Spring can really hang you up the most

WHERE ARE YOU, DARRYL ZANUCK?

Where are you Darryl Zanuck? I've been waiting for your call
Since I was just a teenaged kid and the phone was on the
wall
The rumour should have reached you that in our little
town
A magic, tragic actress lives who's lost and must be found

In a make-believe spotlight my life has been spent
Seems the whole thing has been one long coming event
Now the dream factory's fallen, the studio's gone
And shadows of vultures appear on the lawn

When will I be discovered? Don't leave me to my fate
I'm frightened of my mirror. It's getting awfully late
I know my bloom is fading for time is such a thief
You'll see right through my glasses to the glamour
underneath

There are cries in the distance of panic and war
Come and carry me safe through that magical door
'Cause my whole generation was raised on the dream
That your phone call would come and the angels would
beam

I'm waiting Darryl Zanuck, I wonder where you are
I always knew you'd call some day and then I'd be a star
I'm lonely Darryl Zanuck, I've suffered and I've bled
I wonder if I missed your call. I wonder if you're dead

IT'S ONLY A MOVIE

Don't cry baby, it's only a movie
It's only a picture show
Look and you'll see all the buildings are cardboard
That's only white sugar snow

Don't cry baby, that wound isn't bleeding
It's only tomato sauce
Don't get upset when they're pounding the nails in
It's only a cardboard cross

The wind machine keeps grinding
The thunder's just a drum
The film goes on unwinding
And will till Kingdom come

Don't cry baby, when somebody leaves you
The script called for him to go
Just remember it's only a movie
It's only a picture show

THE THINGS WE NEVER DID

When I think of all the things we never did together
The sunsets and the sights we never shared
I sigh a little sigh, but life speeds right on by
And mocks us for the time we never spared

I remember all the trips we never took together
The trains we missed, the hills we never climbed
I never understood why somehow we never could
And now you're walking ghostly in my mind

Everywhere I wonder, everywhere I roam
All our long lost hours follow me back home

I regret the many talks we never had together
And I'm sorry for the secret selves we hid
Although we rarely meet, it's always bitter sweet
Just to dream of all the things we never did

DREAM LOVE

I dreamt I slipped into your bed
You didn't say I couldn't stay
I had a wooden leg
That made me so ashamed
And then you started stroking it
Your fingers touched the ugly edge
I felt so good
Although I couldn't feel
Your hand
On my wooden leg
I could see that it didn't offend you
"No" you said, "I think it's great"
"I'm glad you like it
'Cause you won't find a girl with one like it"
"I think it's great" you said
As you put your arms around me
And we laughed till we came
I was feeling no pain
And we laughed till we came

WHY

Why is my every love a loss?
Why do our letters always cross?
Why do I always talk too much?
Why does it take so long to touch?

Why is my wisdom just a waste?
Why can't I rest alone and chaste?
Why won't I learn what time has taught?
Why am I always getting caught?

Why do I wear this foolish grin?
What would I do if I should win?
Should I be asking more or less?
Why is my every love a mess?

SONG OF THE PROCRASTINATING PENITENT

When Dante saw the souls in hell
The burning and the frozen
His guide said, "Do not pity them,
Man, that's the scene they've chosen"
The flames of Hades used to wait
For anyone who fell
They must have been brave sinners then
When men believed in hell

Oh Lord I wanna be good
Dear Lord I wanna be good
Sweet Lord I wanna be good
But please not right away

Sometimes I dream there's still a chance
The Devil's gonna get me
I'd like to quit this awful life
But the music just won't let me
I try to keep my hands off you
I try to stay away
But I would gamble all my soul
To have you one more day

Oh Lord I wanna be good
Dear Lord I wanna be good
Good Lord I wanna be good
But please not right away
Sweet Lord I'm gonna be good
Tomorrow not today

The flames of Hades used to wait
For anyone who fell
They must have been brave sinners then
When men believed in hell

SOLSTICE SONG

The year's half gone and what have I done?
I went to Cannes and sat in the sun

The year's half gone and what's there to show?
I fell in love with a man made of snow

The man of snow he melted away
Till I could see his feet were of clay

The time has come for travelling on
I made some love but where has it gone?

I made some songs but where are they sung?
The year's half gone the lady's not young

The year's half gone and I'm still alone
I'm going to see the old druid stones

I'll climb a hill and wait for the dawn
To celebrate the year is half gone

HOMECOMING

Somehow
The birds sound the same
When waking from a dream
In London or in San Francisco

Surely
The cats on the street
Are just as mean or sweet
In London or in San Francisco

So is the smell
Of morning coffee
But the colour
Is different

The grass is the same
It gets you just as high
So is the gossip and the blues
And the boys taste the same
They get you just as high
The only special thing
Is the colour of the sky

MY LOST CITY

My lost city
Smiles in the setting sun
Looking for a moment
As it did when I was young

My Manhattan
Hasn't a chance they say
Still the streets enchant me
On this golden autumn day

Like an old and jaded lady
Paying for her wicked ways
Dreams betrayed and future shady
How I miss those bad old days

Dirty sidewalks
Poisonous air they say
Still I love this city
Just can't seem to stay away

Friends and lovers
Flee from their favourite town
But I will keep returning
Till all the walls fall down

TWILIGHT

If you get through the twilight
You'll live through the night
If you keep off the memories
You'll make it all right

When the city goes slower
And sunset's a ghost
That's the time when a blue mood
Can burn you the most

Draw the curtains, shut out the sky
Call up the boozers, losers and champs
Keep on moving, try to get high
Turn on the music, turn up the lamps

If there's somebody near you
Then just hang on tight
And perhaps you won't fall through
That hole in the night
If you get through the twilight

WHAT ABOUT ME?

When someone's star is beaming
For everyone to see
A silent voice starts screaming
What about me, me, me!
What about me?

And when your love is eyeing
Another form divine
Inside a voice is crying
What about mine, mine, mine!
What about mine?

We all know about oneness
We all know about sharing
We all know so well how it should be
We know the only enemy is ME!

If we could stop those voices
Perhaps we could free
To make some cleaner choices
Than me! me! me!
What about me!
What about me! me! me!
What about me!

ONE DAY AT A TIME

One day at a time, that's how I'm living
One day at a time, that's how I plan
You never can tell what plays tomorrow
I'm ready to move my caravan

One day at a time the world's so pretty
It's looking ahead that makes you tense
You moan about things that never happen
One day at a time makes much more sense

When you look behind or up ahead
You're the seeing blind, the breathing dead
'Cause the thing that matters anyhow
Is the living taste of here and now

One day at a time, that's how I love you
Who knows if my stock will fall or climb
The hours with you, the dream we're dreaming
Can only come true one day at a time

KILLING TIME

Don't blame me for killing time
When time is killing me
I can see him closing in
My ancient enemy

Putting wrinkles in my skin
And eating up my days
Stealing all the rainbow scenes
And leaving weary greys

Don't blame me for filling time
Before a t.v. set
Taking any kind of drug
That helps me to forget

Though tonight you hold me tight
Tonight will always end
Looking in the glass I see
That time is not my friend

Time will carry you away
And show no sympathy
Don't blame me for killing time
When time is killing me

GONE BUT NOT FORGOTTEN

Am I ever gonna touch you
With my message of remorse?
When the ripples finally reach you
Will you recognise the source?
Though I may have made you weary
And I may have made you yawn
Everybody's gonna love me
When at last I'm dead and gone

Will the ones who wandered through me
And passed out the other side
Ever mention that they knew me
With a little touch of pride
Though my act may be too spooky
And too special for today
I've a hunch they're gonna dig it
When at last I pass away

People will go about their business
Sometimes singing my love dreams under their breath
Scholars will write about my legend
I'll be wearing seductive colours of death

Will some housewife washing dishes
As she thinks about my song
Start remembering April wishes
And be sure I wasn't wrong?
Will you listen to my story?
Will you sigh and nod your head?
Will I shine in misty glory
In your memory when I'm dead?

THE "IF" GAME

If you had been . . . if we had seen . . or I knew when . . .
If we had gone three years ago instead of then

If I'd found the time
If you'd really tried
If I could have seen
What you always hide

If we had met . . . If he had come . . If they had said . . .
That plane we missed . . . If you had found . . . If I had
     read . . .

If you hadn't run
If I'd been more free
You wouldn't be you
I wouldn't be me

AM I O.K.?

How am I?
Am I all right? Am I O.K.? Am I just too much?
How am I?
Do I make it? Do you mean it? Will you keep in touch?

How am I? On the level
Am I O.K.? Am I wunderbar?
Tell me why
Am I sunshine? Am I chocolate? Am I superstar?

How can you endure me?
I'm so insecure
When you reassure me
I just ask for more and more

Tell me now
Am I O.K.? Do you dig me? Like a breath of Spring?
Show me how
Am I solid? Am I groovy? Do I really swing?
You're a winner. You're a beauty
And I know you never lie
You're terrific. You're colossal
But, baby, how am I?
Am I O.K.?

SICK CHICKENS

SONG FROM SALVADOR

Soul of the poet haunts the panic's heart
Razors are singing as the teardrops start
Dreams are exploded in the city's face
Monkeys are mourning for the human race

Soft watches watch us as we sing a lie
Dark horsemen catch us though we've learned to fly
White lions meet us in heat of day
Grandmothers greet us when we're far away

Cold soldiers shoot us as we motor west
Vampires eat us as we buy the best
Blue bread awaits us in our mother's arms
White clouds embrace us on our father's farms

Soul of the poet haunts the panic's heart
Razors are singing as the teardrops start
Dreams are exploded in the city's face
Monkeys are mourning for the human race

THE MINISTER OF LUNACY

The Minister of Lunacy has nothing to report
He's permanently out to lunch, his second favourite sport
He's always busy on the phone connecting up with down
His eyes aglow with happy pain like some angelic clown

The people go on wearing socks and eating eggs and spuds
But underneath a crazy beat is throbbing in their blood
They hump and sleep and go to work, they fart and wind
   their clocks
But down below the beat goes on from Mayfair to the docks

The Minister is all shook up, he's gambled with his soul
He wonders where it all went wrong and how he lost control
He hears the sound he fears at last, the music of the bands
The dance macabre that ushers in the final totentanze

The music blasts, the dancers spin, with never any truce
The building shakes, the madness builds, and then
ALL HELL BREAKS LOOSE!
The people tear their clothes and hair and naked each begins
To rip and gouge and maim and maul with idiotic grins

They dance on severed arms and legs like bits of broken toys
A picnic in a slaughterhouse, a stream of blood and noise
And so it is that very few survive the crimson sport
The Minister of Lunacy has nothing to report

KITSCH DEATH

(On the death of a twelve-year-old English girl
at David Cassidy's White City concert)

"She would have wanted it that way"
That's what her parents said
They left her idol's records
Scattered on her little bed

They left her room the way it was
His poster on her wall
She would have wanted it that way
She loved him after all

She went to worship and to scream
With all her little mates
He glittered there upon the stage
Her idol from the States

The crowd pressed closer to the star
It carried her along
In tears she tore her golden hair
Quite maddened by his song

At last he took his final bow
And sadly someone found
A little body lying there
All trampled on the ground

Some wonder if a star is worth
The price such children pay
But we recall her parents' words
"She wanted it that way"

SICK CHICKENS

All our sick chickens
Are coming home to roost
All our queer capons
Are calling for the host
We spend our cravings
And never count the cost
And then one day
We see far away
A tiny speck
That grows in a day
To a great black, nimbus cloud
And it fits us like a shroud

All our sick chickens
Are pecking at the door
All our old dream ways
Are sinking through the floor
We kiss our babies
And never make the beds
And then one day
We hear far away
A tiny buzz
That grows in a day
To a great black crashing sound
And it knocks us to the ground
Where all our old garbage
Is singing with the flies
And all our sick chickens
Start pecking out our eyes

TENNIS, ANYONE? (A TANGO)

We're playing a game of tennis without a ball
In a garden where the flowers never fall
And after the game we'll go in to have our tea
The teacups are empty, so are your eyes on me

We're sitting beside a fire that's never lit
And you hold me but somehow we never fit
You put on a record throbbing with silent drums
And outside the window twilight will never come

I try so hard to reach you
My fingers press your face
But somehow in between us
Are miles and miles of empty space

I'm trying to find some reason for you to stay
But we both admit there's nothing left to say
Your footsteps still echo faintly along the hall
I glance in the mirror, no one is there at all

WHERE THE BLUES BEGIN

Have you come to the place where the days are black
And you've gone too far and you can't come back
And you pitch your tent on a cardboard range
And you sleep with creeps and your friends are strange
And your silver spoon turns to worthless tin?
Then you've come to the place where the blues begin

When there's nothing to do and you've done it twice
And you seem to live in a cave of ice
And you hear no hope in a ringing phone
And you haven't learned how to play alone
When the time is long and the laughs are thin
Then you've come to the place where the blues begin

Once life was funny, free and fast
In every act an all-star cast
They served you first but now you're last
How did you get so old so fast?

When you pray with your lips but the words won't come
And you beg for sleep like a bowery bum
And the hustler stares with his high-speed eyes
And you drown your fear in a glass of lies
When there's nothing left that you care to win
Then you've been to the place where the blues begin
Where the blues begin
Where the blues begin

ALL THAT FALL (FOR ERNIE)

Blessings on the falling humans
Falling man and falling women
All that fall and feel the pain
Surely they will rise again

Blessings on the judge and jailors
Falling hearts and other failures
Dow-Jones Average, falling rain
All that fall will rise again

Blessings on the falling sparrow
Falling snow and falling dollar
Falling hopes and falling nations
All who fall on demonstrations

Blessings on the fallen angels
Falling friends and falling strangers
Falling stars and faithless men
Know dem bones will rise again

PERSONALS

Here in a magazine
Buy it and read
All of the lonely ones
Crying their need
Boy wanted, girl wanted
Man seeking friend
Who ever answers them?
How does it end?

They put their loneliness
Into an ad
Isn't it laughable?
Isn't it sad?
Boy wanted, girl wanted
Longing to meet
Old-fashioned, up-to-date
Clean and discreet

Over-worked investment broker
Planning to relax
Seeking sexy, blonde deduction
From his income tax
Convent-bred, confused young lady
Looking for a guide
Gentleman with private income
Hasn't any pride

Easy to laugh at them
That's understood
You've been the lucky one
You've got it good
Boy wanted, girl wanted
Man seeking friend
Who ever answers them?
How does it end?

INTO THE DARK

The saint and the stripper, the cook and the queen
Some sunset or starset they make the same scene
The cop and the killer, the artist, the clown
They all go into the dark alone

The junkie, the jailor, the old and the young
The hustler, the hooker, the drowned and the hung
My mother, my brother, your lover, your son
They all go into the dark alone

Faces in papers, shadows that danced
Men you admired, girls you romanced
Killer and critic, lover and friend
Everyone all by himself in the end

The fighters and fixers, the fat and the lean
The ladies you lay with, the stars of the screen
The bodies you cherished, the flesh and the bone
They all go into the dark alone

Let's swallow some poison before love is done
We'll fall into darkness and crash on the sun
Then sweetly together we'll move and we'll moan
We won't go into the dark alone

LONDON, WINTER '74

The city's full of secrets
Subversive and insane
The streets are full of killers
Their eyes are full of rain

The parks are full of crazies
Prepared to light the fuse
The trash is full of fingers
That never make the news

The buildings crouch in darkness
Their walls are full of ears
The halls are full of nightmares
The beds are full of tears

The theatre's full of strippers
The churches gasp for breath
The trains are full of plotters
Exchanging maps of death

The streets are full of junkies
Their veins are full of skag
The courts are full of colonels
Who testify in drag

The cars are full of lovers
Like goldfish in their bowls
They bump their heads together
And lick each other's souls

The pubs explode like roses
The coppers hunt for clues
The lovers grab each other
They've got the most to lose

AFTER WE'VE GONE

Who will live in our house
After we've gone
Will they have green plastic
Instead of a lawn?

Who will live in our house
After the wars?
Will there be mutations
That crawl on all fours?

Will the shiny robot workers
Be dreaming strange, new dreams?
Will the pigeons, big as turkeys
Roost on our ancient beams?

Who will use our kitchen?
What will they cook?
Who will sleep in our room
And how will they look?

Will they feel our ghosts disturbing
Their cybernetic years
With the echoes of our laughter
And the shadow of our tears?

Will there still be lovers?
Who will sing our songs?
Who will live in our house
After we've gone?

QUEEN OF HEAVEN

There's a big, black drag-queen in the sky
Smiling down upon us from on high
And we'll all go see her by and by
That big, black drag-queen in the sky

She is waiting on her satin bed
Wearing halos round her kinky head
One fine day she'll give us all the nod
So be prepared to meet your God

She's your killer and your mother
And your baby and your brother
When at last the battle's over
She's your supernatural lover

She will hand us something good to smoke
And we'll see the everlasting joke
Up in heaven we'll be getting high
With that big, black drag-queen in the sky

If you ask her, "Is this all there is?"
She'll say "Honey-pie, it's all showbiz"
And you'll dig it truly, by and by
When you meet that big, black drag-queen in the sky

THE DECLINE OF THE WEST

All the good tunes have been written
All the good songs have been sung
Somewhere a promise was broken
Long ago, when we were young

All the good words have been spoken
All the good wars have been fought
All the good scenes have been stolen
The big fish have all been caught

All the good weekends are over
All the good games have been played
May as well stay with your lover
The good moves have all been made

All of our bridges are burning
All the good songs have been sung
Somewhere we took the wrong turning
Long ago when we were young

NOT WITH A BANG

Not with a bang but a whimper
Not with a sword but a pin
That's how the ending will find me
Here with my white Gunga Din

Sex I recall was enthralling
But there was always a catch
I found my way in the darkness
Not with a torch but a match

Soon I'll be making my exit
Leaving my room in a mess
Not with a bang but a whimper
Dead I'm still not a success

I'll sleep at last in my coffin
Worn out but not very old
Dead not of terminal cancer
Only a very bad cold